SCHOLASTIC

K SuperSkills

Recognizing Words

PLUS

- Letters & Sounds
- Alphabet
- Rhyming Words
- Drawing & Writing

by Ellen Booth Church

Copyright © 1996 by Scholastic Inc.
Illustrations copyright © 1996 by Scholastic Inc.
All rights reserved. Published by Scholastic Inc.
Printed in the U.S.A.
ISBN 0-590-97700-8

1   2   3   4   5   6   7   8   9   10   02   01   00   99   98   97   96

Scholastic Inc.
New York Toronto London Auckland Sydney

A Message to Parents

Welcome to the fun!

Dear Parents,

Welcome to the fun! Why do children love mazes and "what's wrong here?" pictures? They love the challenge! These activities use visual and motor skills that are essential to reading and writing.

Kindergartners also love to play with sounds and words. Your child may enjoy making up matching sounds or even invented words that rhyme. Reading and writing also use auditory skills. Play and practice with letter sounds and rhyming link a visual image (a letter or word) and the sound it makes. Some children are naturals at auditory skills, while others need practice. But all children enjoy the fun of listening for matching sounds.

You will notice a blend of visual and auditory skills in this book. Reading and writing use both. A good balance of these skills helps your child develop a storehouse of strategies to use in reading.

Recognizing Words provides fun and practice with a progression of essential reading and writing skills. The activities are organized by concept: *sequencing, visual discrimination, alphabet,* and *letters and sounds.* Each section provides a range of skill levels, so your child experiences increasing challenges.

Many activities have more than one "right" answer. Some ask your child to "look again." This open-ended approach allows children to work at their own level and to feel successful. Keep it playful! Try the following activities, and enjoy reading together every day. Have fun, and remember, thinking <u>really</u> <u>is</u> child's play!

Ellen Booth Church

Ellen Booth Church

Reading & Writing Every Day!

Children learn by doing. Here are simple activities to develop reading and writing skills in everyday life:

Visual/Motor Skills

• Writing uses both visual and physical skills. Mazes invite children to develop these skills. Start big … create a maze of furniture or boxes for your child to move through! Then make a drawing of the maze you created together.

• While riding in the car or waiting at an appointment, draw simple spirals and jagged-line mazes for your child to play and write in. Then invite your child to make one for you to fill in!

Rhyming

• Children love to play with the sounds of words. Play a game of real and pretend words that rhyme. You can start with your child's name and make up words that rhyme with it.

Familiar Words

• In the neighborhood, at the store, or at school, look for words like *stop* and *go*, *up* and *down*, *in* and *out*.

• Suggest that your child use familiar words to label your home. Together, write familiar words on paper or file cards. Then post them around your home. Doors can be marked *in* and *out*, stairs *up* and *down*. Items can be labeled with their names: *sink, tub, toy box.*

Creative Writing

• Invite your child to draw pictures to tell a story. Suggest that she can write the story her own way, or you can write her dictated story for her. Do not correct writing or grammar. It is important for your child to express thoughts freely.

• Provide a hard-covered notebook for your child to keep a journal. She can put interesting found objects in her journal, postcards from trips, ticket stubs, photos, or whatever is important to her. On other pages she can draw and write about things she is thinking about and feeling. You will save the journal for years to come!

How Can I Go?

Help each bug find its way to other bugs just like it.

For Grown-Ups

Doing mazes prepares your child for reading and writing by developing a sense of directionality on the page. As you and your child help the bugs find their way through the maze, make up stories about them!

RITA LASCARO

I Don't Want to Be Late

Find different ways for this girl to get to school. Which way is fastest?

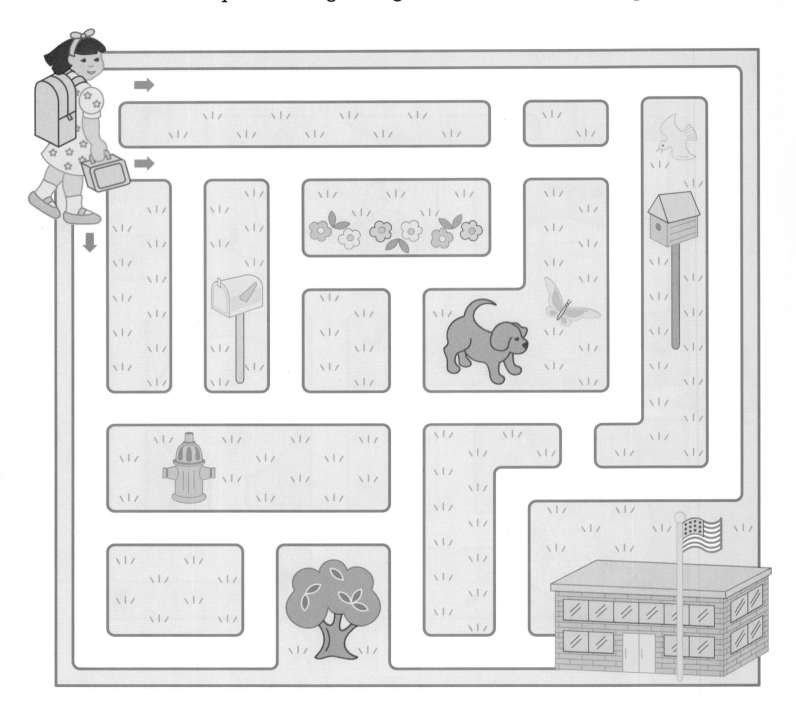

For Grown-Ups

How many ways to school can you and your child find? How did you decide which way was the fastest? Investigate superlatives—biggest, longest, heaviest, fastest. "That is the biggest cat I've seen. This is the longest truck."

Find the Flowers

Which way should the animals go?

For Grown-Ups

Together, guide the animals to the flowers. Use directional words as you move your finger through the maze. Find ways around obstacles. Who gets there the quickest? You may enjoy creating your own nature maze with sticks and rocks!

WILL HILLENBRAND

What's the Story?

This story is written with pictures. Can you tell what it says?

For Grown-Ups

Interpreting pictures and telling a story based on them are activities that develop logic, oral language, and understanding of story structure. For fun, try making your own picture symbols and using them to create a story together.

BARBARA GRAY

Make a Story!
Draw. Cut and paste. Tell your story.

For Grown-Ups

Your child may want to draw pictures for a story, or you might help cut and paste the pictures to create a tale.
Then ask your child to tell you the whole story. You can enjoy drawing and telling stories anytime!

Alphabet Roller-Coaster

Write the missing letters. Draw pictures of things that start with the letters

Aa Bb Cc Dd Ee Ff Gg Hh Ii Jj Kk Ll

For Grown-Ups

Use the pages to play an alphabet game with your child. Say, "A is for *ant*."
Then invite your child to identify the next item in the train. Take turns going from α to z.

Mm Nn Oo Pp Qq Rr Ss Tt Uu Vv Ww Xx Yy Zz

Tidy Tom's Toys!

Tom only likes toys that start with Tt.
What goes in Tom's toy box? Draw lines. Write the letter.

Tom's _oys

For Grown-Ups

Develop familiarity with the letter and sound Tt by pretending that Tom only likes things that start with Tt. Find objects in your house that Tom might have. Draw a picture of Tom's house. Decorate with the things you found together.

Fill Fran's Basket

Fran found five things that start with Ff.
Draw lines. Put them in her basket. Write the letter.

Fran's
_ishing
Basket

For Grown-Ups

Ask what your child would give Fran for a birthday present. (Hint: Fran's gifts always start with Ff!) After your child draws pictures of some presents, try to guess what they are.

What's Happening?

Circle seven or more things that start with Hh.
Write the letter. Tell a story about the picture.

For Grown-Ups

What in the world is happening in the picture? Listen as your child tells you the story. Encourage him or her to use words that begin with Hh. Each of you can add to the story by adding one more thing that starts with Hh!

Glory's Garden Is Growing!

Circle at least seven things that start with Gg. Write the letter.
Put an X on something that grows in Glory's garden.

KEEP OFF
THE
_ RASS

CHRIS DEMAREST

For Grown-Ups

Reinforce letter-sound correspondence by pointing to objects and inviting your child to name them and tell which ones start with Gg. Make a list of things that start with Gg! Note that *giraffe* and some other words have a different Gg sound.

Bakery Sounds

Some things near a box start with Bb. Some things start with Ss. Write the letter for the sound in each box. You can also cut and paste

For Grown-Ups

Pretend you own the "B Bakery." You only sell bakery goods that begin with Bb. Your child can pretend to be a customer and order items. Switch roles. Your child owns the "S Grocery," which only sells things beginning with Ss.

Pat the Cat

Say the cat's name. Draw lines from the cat
to things that rhyme. Fill in the missing letters.

__at

__at

Welcome __at

__at

PAT

__at

For Grown-Ups

Help your child learn sound discrimination and rhyming words. Make up silly sentences together!
Choose real and made-up words that rhyme with *Pat* to use in your silly sentences.

CLAUDE MARTINOT

Seaside Fun!

Circle the things that rhyme with **bug**.

For Grown-Ups

Encourage your child to use the rhyming words to make up a story about the bug. You might want to start by asking, "Would you like to hug a bug?" Your child may enjoy your help in illustrating the story.

17

You're the Cook!

Read the recipe. Put a ✔ on the fruits you need.
What can you make with the things that are left over?

Fruit Salad

1 apple   1 peach

1 banana   1 orange

1 pear   1 strawberry

1 plum   1 melon

grapes

Slice. Mix. Eat!

For Grown-Ups

As your child checks off items, you might each put a finger on the letters and spell each word together. This helps with understanding that letters make up a word, and with word recognition. You may wish to make the fruit salad together!

Time to Move

What has been moved out of the house?
Put a ✔ next to each thing on the list.

chair
lamp
table
television
rocking chair
bed
couch

For Grown-Ups

After you have matched the words, play a matching game! Together, make a list of furniture in your own home. Write the same words in a second column on the page, but in different order. Invite your child to draw lines to match words.

Stop and Go

Circle **stop** and **go** in the picture. Put a ✔ next to anything that stops.
Put an X on anything that goes.

Go to George's for great goodies

Stop in at Stella's

For Grown-Ups

This activity helps your child recognize words she or he may see in the environment. Talk about where you see STOP signs and where you see the word *go*. Try spotting STOP and GO signs when you are out walking or driving.

BARBARA GRAY

Color the Cans

Draw lines to put the paint cans on the shelf.

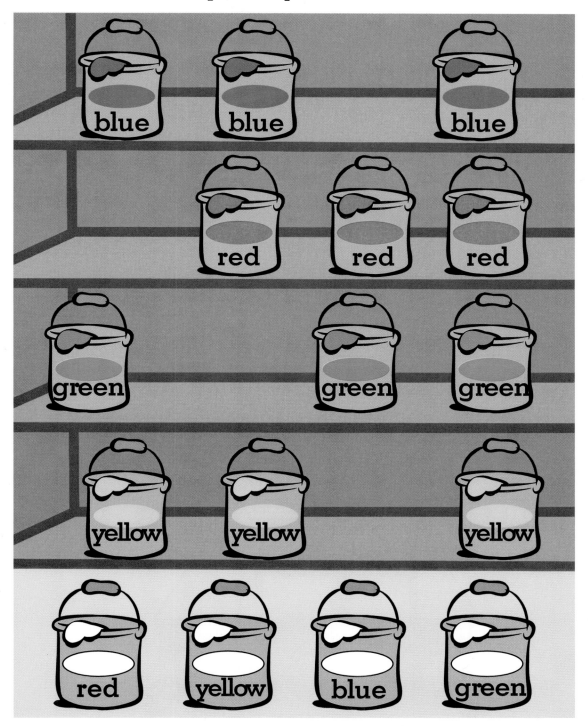

For Grown-Ups

Learning color words gives your child a sense of mastery. Design a house on paper together. Show an inside view, like an open doll house. Ask your child to dictate or write color names. Then "paint" the rooms with crayons.

Who's in the Doghouse?

Fill in the letters. Cut out the dogs.
Paste them **in** and **out** of the doghouses.

in

out

_ut

_n

_n

For Grown-Ups

To build knowledge of these words, play an "In and Out" game. Use a small rug or a circle made with yarn for the "in" space. Make "in" and "out" cards. As you hold up a card, your child jumps in or out of the space.

TERESA ANDERKO

Going Up, Coming Down

Cut out the hikers. Paste them where they belong. Fill in the letters.

For Grown-Ups

Help your child cut the vertical strip from the page, and then cut out each hiker. To develop the concepts, talk about other things people go up and down, such as ladders, escalators, and stairs. Make a ramp and roll toy cars up and down!

CLAUDE MARTINOT

23

What Shall I Take?

Pretend you are going exploring. Where will you go?
Who will go with you? Draw something you will take.

For Grown-Ups

Encourage your child to tell you about the imaginary journey she or he planned. Describing a trip and things to take develops oral language, story creation, and logical thinking. Your child may want to write a label for the drawing.

What Is Your Dream?

Draw what you see in your dream.

For Grown-Ups

Invite your child to tell you about the drawing and to dictate a sentence for you to write if he or she wishes. Or your child may wish to label the drawing. Drawing and speaking about ideas brings your child closer to written language.

What's the Problem?

How would you solve the problem? Draw a picture.

For Grown-Ups

This activity invites logical thinking and expression. Act out the scenario together, using the solution your child drew. Help your child think of alternative endings to act out and discuss. Which ending was most satisfactory to everyone?

What Would You Do?

Draw a picture to show what you would do.

For Grown-Ups

This activity encourages constructive, logical thinking and expression. Make a list together of "problem solvers." Encourage your child to think of people who can help with problems such as getting locked out or having a broken TV.

Rhyme Time!

Cut out the cards. Say the name of each picture.
Use the cards to play games. Make up your own rhyme games!

The Memory Game

Spread the cards face down on a table or floor.
Choose two cards. Do you have a rhyming match?
If not, turn the cards over. Keep trying until all the cards are matched.

Silly Sentences

Choose two rhyming cards. Make up funny sentences using the
rhyming words. Try making a sentence with three rhyming cards.
Can you make a silly sentence using <u>four</u> rhyming cards?

The big pig did a jig

For Grown-Ups

Have fun playing the "Memory Game" together. Share your strategies for remembering the cards. What is the longest rhyming sentence you can make together? Repeat it together until your child can say it from memory!

"What's the Word?" Lotto

Cut out the cards. Match the words. Put the cards on the board.

cat	stop	out
up	red	go
king	blue	in
yellow	down	green

For Grown-Ups

You may wish to laminate the page before cutting. Enjoy the lotto word game with your child. To enrich vocabulary, make up sentences using the words you match. You can also use the picture cards from page 32 with this game board.

stop

blue

king

yellow

out

red

| up | green | cat | in | down | go |

RANDY CHEWNING

More Word Lotto!

Cut out the cards. Match pictures with words.

For Grown-Ups

You may wish to laminate the page before cutting. After playing picture lotto, try using the word cards from page 31 with this game board. You can also use the picture cards on the word game board. Which game is your child's favorite?

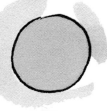

32